DATE DUE

oct			

TURTLES

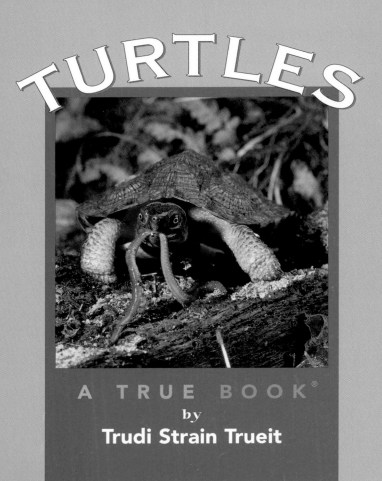

A TRUE BOOK®

by

Trudi Strain Trueit

Children's Press®
A Division of Scholastic Inc.

New York Toronto London Auckland Sydney
Mexico City New Delhi Hong Kong
Danbury, Connecticut

A Geoffrey's sideneck turtle and butterflies

Reading Consultant
Nanci R. Vargus, Ed.D.
*Assistant Professor
Literacy Education
University of Indianapolis
Indianapolis, IN*

Content Consultant
Joseph T. Collins
*Director, The Center for North
American Herpetology
Lawrence, Kansas*

Dedication:
For my niece, Trina, with love

Library of Congress Cataloging-in-Publication Data

Trueit, Trudi Strain.
    Turtles / by Trudi Strain Trueit.
        p. cm. – (A True book)
    Includes bibliographical references and index.
    ISBN 0-516-22652-5 (lib. bdg.)   0-516-29352-4 (pbk.)
    1. Turtles—Juvenile literature. [1. Turtles.] I. Title. II. Series.
QL666.C5T77 2003
597.92—dc21

                                                                2002005880

Contents

A spotted turtle
in a pond

Timeless Turtles

Turtles have lived on Earth for a very long time. More than 200 million years ago, turtles shared the planet with dinosaurs. Today, there are about 280 different kinds of turtles.

Two-thirds of all turtles make their homes in fresh water such as ponds, lakes, and rivers.

Turtles that swim in the ocean are known as sea turtles. Turtles that live only on land are often called tortoises. You can find turtles just about everywhere on Earth, except Antarctica. It is too cold for turtles to live there.

Turtles are ectotherms (ECK-tuh-therms). This means that they rely on their **environments** to warm and cool their bodies. Turtles **bask** in the sun to get warm.

Turtles basking in the sun

To cool off, they rest in the shade. Leatherback sea turtles are different because their muscles make heat while they swim. This heat, along with a thick layer of fat, lets them travel into colder waters, where other turtles cannot go.

Leatherbacks are the largest turtles in the world. They can grow to be 8 feet (2.4 meters) long and can weigh up to 1,900 pounds (862 kilograms). The speckled cape tortoise is

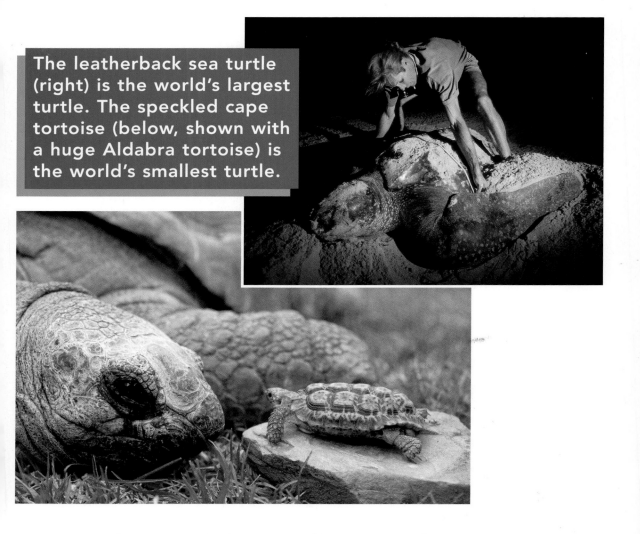

The leatherback sea turtle (right) is the world's largest turtle. The speckled cape tortoise (below, shown with a huge Aldabra tortoise) is the world's smallest turtle.

the world's smallest turtle. Its shell measures just over 3 inches (8 centimeters) in length.

Home in a Shell

All turtles have shells. The top part of the shell is called the carapace (CARE-uh-pass). The underside is called the plastron. The carapace and plastron are connected to one another. Openings are left for the head, tail, and four legs. A turtle's rib cage and backbone are attached

carapace

plastron

These photographs show a turtle's carapace (above) and plastron (left).

to its shell. That is why you will never see a turtle leave its shell behind.

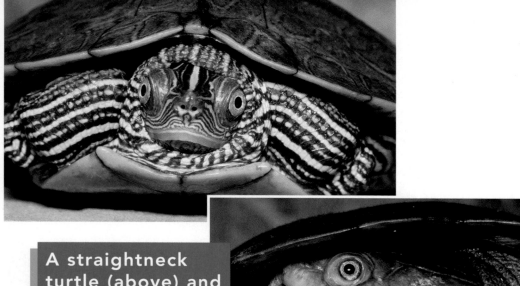

A straightneck turtle (above) and a sideneck turtle (right)

Straightneck turtles pull their heads directly into their shells using an up-and-down S motion. Sideneck turtles tuck their heads sideways to fit under the rims of their shells.

A turtle's shell is made of bone and is covered with a layer of horny scales called scutes (skoots). The scutes are made of **keratin** (CARE-uh-tin), the same material that is in your fingernails.

Most kinds of turtles have bony shells covered with scutes.

A typical turtle has fifty-four scutes—thirty eight on its carapace and sixteen on its plastron. Softshell, pig-nosed, and leatherback turtles have leathery skin instead of scutes.

A softshell turtle

You can tell a lot about how a turtle lives by its shell. The smooth, flat, teardrop-shaped shell of the leatherback helps it dive 3,000 feet (914 m) underwater. Tortoises have heavy, domed shells that protect them from the sun.

Some turtles, such as painted turtles, spotted turtles, and sliders, have shells marked with bright stripes, dots, and other patterns. But most turtle shells are dull green, black, or brown. These colors act as **camouflage**

16

(CAM-uh-flawj). They help the turtle blend into its surroundings so **predators** and **prey** cannot see it.

South America's matamata turtle has loose flaps of skin that float in the water. The flaps look just like dead leaves. They attract

A matamata turtle underwater

A musk turtle

fish, which the matamata then sucks into its mouth. Musk and mud turtles often resemble rocks in the bottom of a pond. If bothered, they may bite or give off a terrible scent. Musk turtles are also called "stinkpots."

Box It Up!

Most turtles can withdraw into their shells when they sense danger. If you hear a hissing sound, it is air escaping from the turtle's lungs to make room inside the shell for its head, tail, and legs.

A box turtle is expert at hiding inside its armored shell. A special hinge divides its plastron into two movable parts. Using powerful muscles, the box turtle can seal off every opening so tightly that not even strong predators such as raccoons and foxes can pry its shell open.

A Turtle's Senses

A 200-pound (91-kg) alligator snapping turtle lies very still in a pond. Its mouth is open wide and a little pink lure on its tongue is wriggling. To a curious fish, the lure looks like a worm. The fish grabs for the "worm." Snap! The turtle clamps its powerful jaws shut

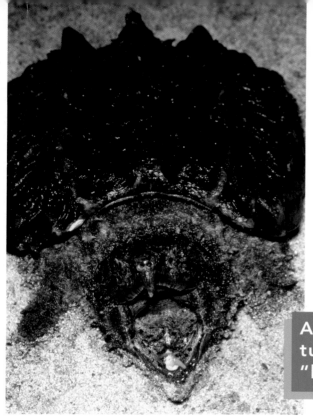

An alligator snapping turtle showing the "lure" on its tongue

and swallows its dinner whole. Snapping turtles eat whatever they can catch, including fish, frogs, ducks, and small animals. Most turtles eat plants, insects, worms, snails, and fish.

Tortoises usually munch on plants, fruits, or dead animals. Sea turtles prefer grass, crabs, and oysters. Sometimes leatherbacks mistake plastic bags for their favorite food, jellyfish. They may swallow the bags and die.

Turtles do not have teeth. Instead, sharp edges along their inner jaws cut and tear food. That is why you should never handle musk, box, or snapping turtles. Snapping turtles have been known to snap broom handles in half with their jaws!

The sharp edges of a turtle's jaws help the turtle cut and tear food.

A turtle's shell, tail, and feet are sensitive to touch. Tortoises have five toes on each foot that are attached like an elephant's. Tortoises are the slowest turtles. They travel at less than 0.3 miles (0.5 kilometers) per hour, which means it would probably take a tortoise more than 3 hours to travel 1 mile (1.6 km).

Freshwater turtles have separate toes and claws, often with webbing between them. Sea turtles have paddlelike flippers with two, one, or no claws.

The feet of a Galápagos tortoise (top) and a freshwater turtle (middle) are very different. Sea turtles have flippers that help them "fly" through the water (bottom).

On the beach, sea turtles are clumsy. But in the ocean, they can zip through the water at speeds up to 15 miles (24 km) per hour.

Turtles usually have good vision. Sea turtles can see well underwater, but can see only short distances on land.

Turtles have a strong sense of smell. A special sensory organ in a turtle's nose called a Jacobson's organ helps it detect smells in the air.

Turtles have good vision and a keen sense of smell.

Turtles do not have ears on the outsides of their heads. An inner eardrum picks up low sounds and vibrations from the ground and water.

Family Life

During mating season, several male turtles may fight over a female. They bite each other's carapaces to win her. Turtles may mate on land or in the water. After mating, all turtles nest on land—even sea turtles. Sea turtles may travel more than 3,000 miles (4,828 km) to return

Male desert tortoises fighting during mating season (above) and a map turtle laying an egg in a nest (left)

to the beach where they were born to make their own nests.

Most female turtles build a nest by digging a pit in the dirt or sand with their hind legs. All turtles lay eggs. Africa's pancake tortoise lays just one egg but may do so several times a year. A sea turtle lays between eighty and two hundred eggs at a time.

Once the eggs are laid, the mother buries the nest. The babies are left to hatch on their own, usually in a few months. When it is ready to be born, a hatchling cracks its eggshell open with a special "egg tooth" on its snout. At birth, a hatchling's carapace is barely bigger than a quarter.

Newly hatched loggerhead sea turtles heading for the safety of the sea

Eggs and baby turtles are in constant danger. Raccoons, opossums, foxes, and other predators raid turtle nests to eat the eggs. Humans dig up turtle eggs for food. Tiny hatchlings are prey for birds,

Mammals and birds may raid turtle nests for the eggs.

bears, skunks, and coyotes. Baby sea turtles are attacked by sea birds, sharks, fish, and otters. Scientists say that only about one in every hundred turtle hatchlings will reach adulthood. For sea turtles, that number may be as low as one in every thousand.

Slow Turtle, Long Life

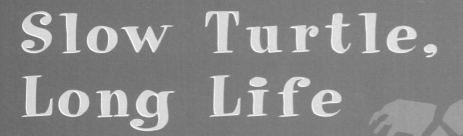

Turtles have long lives. Freshwater turtles may live to be 40 years old and sea turtles may live longer than 80 years. Tortoises win the race for the longest life span. In the wild, they can live to be 150 years old— and in **captivity**, they have been known to live even longer!

An Aldabra giant tortoise can live to be more than 100 years old.

Turtle Rescue

In the last few centuries, turtles have faced their fiercest predators of all—humans. Early whalers hunted some kinds of giant tortoises of the Galápagos (Gah-LAH-puh-goss) Islands to **extinction**. Once numbering in the hundreds of thousands, now less than fifteen thousand giant tortoises remain.

The radiated tortoise (left) and the hawksbill sea turtle (below) are among the turtles that are in danger of becoming extinct.

Today, more than twenty types of turtles around the world are endangered. This means that their populations are so low that they could become extinct at any time.

Turtles face many dangers. They are often killed for their oil, meat, shells, and skins. The hawksbill sea turtle is hunted for its beautiful scutes, which are turned into jewelry. Many sea turtles, such as Kemp's ridleys and

A hawksbill sea turtle caught in a shrimping net

loggerheads, get tangled in shrimping nets. Unable to swim to the surface for air, they drown.

Humans also destroy turtle habitats. Wetlands are drained so cities can expand. Sea turtle nesting sites are crowded out by beach houses. Pollution poisons the oceans, rivers, and lakes where turtles live.

People are starting to realize that if turtles are to have a future, we must help them. Many nations, including the United States, have made it illegal to hunt turtle eggs. It is also against the law to kill threatened and endangered turtles such as sea turtles, Galápagos giant tortoises, and many other kinds of tortoises and turtles.

In the United States, shrimp fishers must use a turtle excluding device (TED). This is a metal cage that safely releases turtles that get caught in fishing nets. **Conservationists** have set up programs to monitor sea-turtle nesting sites. The

Shrimp fishermen holding up a net with a turtle excluding device

These conservationists are moving sea turtle eggs from a public beach to a safer nesting site.

nests may be dug up and the eggs relocated to a safe hatchery beach. Once the babies are born, they are returned to their home shore, where they are protected as they scurry for the water.

It may take many years before some turtle populations are out of trouble. Through care, conservation, and worldwide cooperation, we can make sure these long-lived creatures continue to live on.

To Find Out More

Here are some additional resources to help you learn more about turtles:

 **Books**

Arnosky, Jim. **All About Turtles.** Scholastic Inc., 2000.

Baskin-Salzberg, Anita and Allan Salzberg. **Turtles.** Franklin Watts, 1996.

Blair, Diane and Pamela Wright. **Sea Turtle Watching: A How-to Guide.** Capstone Books, 2000.

Miller, Sara Swan. **Turtles: Life in a Shell.** Franklin Watts, 1999.

Schafer, Susan. **Turtles.** Benchmark Books, 1999.

Thomas, Peggy. **Reptile Rescue.** Twenty-first Century Books, 2000.

Organizations and Online Sites

Center for Marine Conservation

1725 DeSales Street
N.W.,Suite 600
Washington, DC 20036
http://www.cmc-ocean.org

This organization helps preserve ocean habitats through research and education. Its website includes games, puzzles, and activities that show how humans can keep the oceans healthy for sea turtles and other marine life.

Sea Turtle Survival League Caribbean Conservation Corporation

4424 NW 13th St. Suite #A-1
Gainesville, FL 32609
http://www.cccturtle.org

Learn about the different types of sea turtles, see video clips, and discover how you can get involved in protecting these endangered turtles and their habitats.

Tortoise Trust USA

PMB #292
685 Bridge Street Plaza
Owatonna, MN 55060
http://www.tortoisetrust.org

This organization works to protect turtles and provide information on the proper care of captive turtles. At the website you can also explore the image gallery to see amazing photos of turtles such as the star tortoise and ornate box turtle.

U.S. Fish and Wildlife Service Endangered Species Program

4401 N. Fairfax Drive,
Room 420
Arlington, VA 22203
http://endangered.fws.gov/
kids/index.html

This government agency works to conserve, protect, and enhance wildlife populations. The FWS website offers current listings of threatened and endangered turtles, along with tips on how you can help protect turtles and other wildlife in your community.

Important Words

bask warm the body by lying in the sun

camouflage way an animal uses its body color and texture to blend in with its surroundings

captivity state of being kept and cared for by humans

conservationists people who help preserve and protect wildlife

environments surroundings of living things

extinction death of a species of animal or plant

keratin strong material that forms the horns, claws, nails, and scales of turtles

predators animals that hunt other animals for food

prey animals hunted by other animals for food

Index

Meet the Author

Trudi Strain Trueit is an award-winning television news reporter who has contributed stories to *ABC News*, *CBS News*, and *CNN*. Ms. Trueit has written many books for Scholastic on weather, nature, and wildlife. She is the author of three other books in the True Book series: *Alligators and Crocodiles*, *Lizards*, and *Snakes*.

Ms. Trueit recently saw her first Pacific ridley sea turtle. Although these turtles prefer the warm waters off Mexico, an injured female ridley with a broken shell came ashore on the Washington coast. She was rescued for rehabilitation at the Seattle Aquarium and was eventually returned to the wild.

Ms. Trueit lives in Everett, Washington, with her husband, Bill, a high-school computer teacher.